SENIOR MOMENTS

Joey Green and Alan Corcoran

A Fireside Book
Published by Simon & Schuster
New York   London   Toronto   Sydney

FIRESIDE
Rockefeller Center
1230 Avenue of the Americas
New York, NY 10020

Designed by William Ruoto

For information regarding special discounts for bulk purchases, please contact Simon & Schuster
Special Sales at 1-800-456-6798 or business@simonandschuster.com

Manufactured in the United States of America

10   9

Library of Congress Cataloging-in-Publication Data
Green, Joey.
Senior moments / Joey Green and Alan Corcoran.
p. cm.
"A Fireside book."
1. Aging—Humor. I. Corcoran, Alan. II. Title.
PN6231.A43 G74 2002
818'.5402—dc21   2002067519

ISBN 0-7432-2696-8

for our parents

Introduction

Y ou need three pairs of glasses to get through the morning paper. Your old friends are dropping like flies. On a good day, nothing hurts until your medication wears off. You've hit the golden years, but it feels more like an episode of the Twilight Zone.

Well, fear not. You're not alone. Senior citizens are the fastest growing segment of the population. Thirty-nine million Americans are over the age of 65. In fact, someone turns 65 in the United States every fourteen seconds. Like you, they're not too happy about it either—unless you're overjoyed that you're now entitled to a senior citizen discount on a cup of coffee at McDonald's.

Okay, so you can no longer remember your own phone number and you're constantly driving home to the wrong house. You haven't lost your marbles. You're simply having a few Senior Moments. Savor them, treasure them, and above all, get used to them. Experts are projecting that 100th birthday parties are becoming as common as liver spots. You're going to be in this state of confusion for some time to come, so you might as well sit back, relax, and smell the Geritol.

And so, as a public service, we've prepared this checklist of Senior Moments (in large print for your convenience) to reassure you that you haven't gone senile. You're simply experiencing a second childhood. Just be careful. It's a proven fact that too many birthdays can kill you.

SENIOR
MOMENTS

Your salary was once ten bucks cash a week, and you paid only a dime in Federal taxes.

All the names in your
little black book are doctors.

You had to install an
auxiliary medicine cabinet.

When you say, "Over my dead body!" people aren't sure if you're kidding.

You haven't had a "six-pack"
of either kind since the
Eisenhower administration.

You're pretty sure you can duplicate
a home-theater system by turning up
the sound on your RCA console.

You think you know the difference
between a CD and a DVD,
but you don't own any.

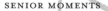

You did not see any movie nominated
for an Academy Award last year.

You remember when a
"subway series" was played between
the New York Giants and
the Brooklyn Dodgers.

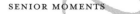

You've argued that the forward pass
ruined the game of football.

Whenever anyone says that
the circumstances that caused the
Great Depression can never happen
again, you remember that
this is precisely what they said
the first time around.

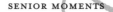

You liked the movies better when
the actors didn't talk.

You'd still change your own oil
if you could figure out
how to reach the hood release.

You can't read a map
with your driving glasses,
but you can still
fold it like a pro.

Your video camera died, but your
8mm movie camera still works fine.

Most of your "camping" gear
was first used in WWII.

You have a 1980 car with
10,000 miles on it.

You've pre-purchased a coffin.

You'll take Betty Grable over Madonna any day of the week.

When people tell you
"You can't take it with you!"
they really mean
"Give me some of it now!"

You got home from the airport
to discover your car was stolen
—until the cops found it right where
you parked it at the airport.

The only people who refer
to heart attacks as "mild"
are people who
have never had one.

You can hear just fine—you just can't
make out what people are saying.

After you spend a half hour
frantically searching for your bifocals,
your wife informs you that
they are on top of your head.

You are startled back to reality by the sound of someone saying, "Hello?" —and then realize you have no idea who you just called or why.

You have an unfortunate tendency
to address your children
using the dog's name.

You are delighted to discover that
your new acquaintance is taking
all of the same prescriptions you are.

When you finish your shopping trip
at the local mega-mall, you have
no idea where you parked the car
or which car you took.

Your short-term memory
has been replaced
by a pad and pencil,
but you can't remember
where you put the pad.

You turn on the TV to find out what the date is—and then check to see if you are reading today's newspaper.

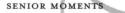

When you stand
at the foot of the stairs,
you can't remember whether
you're about to go up for something
or whether you just came down.

You've eaten dinner before 3 P.M.
to get the Early Bird Special.

You hope to find a long line
at the Post Office or bank
so you'll have something to do.

You haven't been on a roller coaster
in thirty years.

You refuse to buy a cellular phone.

When you're standing with a group
of friends and someone drops a pen,
no one bends down to pick it up.

You've fallen asleep in a
Dunkin' Donuts.

Your cardiologist looks like a
Cub Scout.

Now that you have
all the time in the world to
put your snapshots in photo albums,
you have no idea who the
people in the photos are.

You drove to 7-Eleven,
stepped inside and then couldn't
remember why.

All you talk about are your
aches and pains.

When your leg falls asleep,
you can't wake it up.

You shop for Metamucil at Costco.

You're on a first-name basis with a pharmacist.

You've thrown out your back
opening a can of tuna fish
—with an electric can opener.

You once owned a Beatles wig.

You've got a beer belly and
you don't drink beer.

You know who Jack Benny and
Rochester were.

You get more get-well cards
than bills.

You know the difference between a gastroenterologist, oncologist, and otolaryngologist.

You actually enjoy playing canasta,
mah johng, and bridge.

When you light
the candles on your birthday cake,
the smoke alarm goes off.

You dig shuffleboard.

You know what the D in D-Day stands for.

You're more interested in
catching the Early Bird Special
than the Late Late Show.

You'd rather save 30 cents off a
canister of Quaker Oats
than save the world.

You had your inner child
surgically removed.

"Giving it the old college try" now means "taking an incomplete."

You know who Jack Dempsey was.

You've thanked heaven for Depends.

The senior citizens
in television commercials
look twenty years younger
than you do.

You've been banned for life
from the nude beach.

You thought Frank Sinatra
was a punk.

You know that
"You'll probably outlive all of us!"
really means "I'm glad I'm not
as close to death as you are!"

The last time you surfed online
to add to your CD collection,
you snapped up a nice 3-month
maturity with a tasty 7.25 APR
—all for a measly $10,000.

You're fully aware that there is
nothing Modern about Maturity.

Making the faces and numbers larger on U.S. currency was a good start, but they should print the bills in different colors, too.

Somewhere in your house,
you still have a drawer filled with
spare tubes and fuses.

On your college football team
only sissies wore helmets.

You have never called anyone collect.

You hated *The Golden Girls.*

You were nominated as "Class Chair"
for your 50th college reunion
—by both of your surviving classmates.

You have used the phrase,
"I have socks older than you"
—and you weren't kidding.

When people complain about
how bad the Seventies were,
you wish they had been around
for the Thirties.

If you really followed
your doctor's orders,
you would have lost
the will to live.

"I knew Spring Chicken,
Spring Chicken was a friend of mine,
and sir, you are no Spring Chicken!"

You can nap at the drop of a hat.

You don't want anything for
Christmas.

Job interviewers no longer ask you "Where do you think you will be in five years?"

You have your own phone number
written down somewhere.

You can't get through an entire
Oliver Stone movie without
at least one bathroom break.

You can no longer differentiate
your dreams from reality.

You know how to do the Charleston,
the Jitterbug, and the Lindy.

You can sing "Mairzy Doats."

You ask for a doggy bag at Denny's.

You went to your 50th high school reunion and thought you accidentally stepped into a convalescent home.

You know seven "cures" for arthritis.

You need a magnifying glass to read
a stop sign.

You sit at the head of the table.

Your gynecologist went to high school
with your son.

You wish you knew how to read lips.

Your Social Security number is 27.

You invite door-to-door salesmen
into your home because
you enjoy the company.

Your freckles
have turned into sunspots,
one of which resembles
a map of Texas.

You've realized that old age is
better than the alternative.

You've realized that you haven't
just mellowed with age,
you're growing mold.

You have constant jet lag—
without flying.

You remember the advent of nylon.

You subscribe to the large-print
edition of *Reader's Digest*
but you still can't understand why
the words look so fuzzy.

You still have a leisure suit
hanging in your closet.

Your hair is blue.

You know how to make bathtub gin.

You remember life before
Mickey Mouse.

Happy Hour is a nap.

You have a recurring nightmare that your children are putting you in a home where you're fed nothing but rice pudding and Jell-O cubes.

You remember the popularity of the martini.

Your dreams are reruns.

You think the
President of
the United States
is just some dumb kid.

You've realized that toupees
only fool people
who wear them.

You've accidentally opened
your outgoing mail.

You fear a surprise party
might kill you.

You listened to "The Shadow."

The picture in your passport is by Leonardo Da Vinci.

There's a box of pitted prunes
in your pantry.

You've come to the conclusion that gravity gets stronger as you get older.

All your food is salt-free, fat-free, cholesterol-free, and taste-free.

You've spent your
entire Social Security check
at the slot machines
on a Caribbean cruise ship.

Your children collect
Social Security.

You can knit a sweater.

The print in newspapers
seems to be
getting smaller.

You ask for a senior citizen discount
on McDonald's coffee.

Suits and dresses magically
shrink in your closet.

You think Betty White still looks like
one hot mama.

You owned a zoot suit.

Your grandson is bald.

When your spouse whispers sweet nothings in your ear, that's exactly what you hear —nothing.

The word "regular" has taken on
a whole new meaning.

You've accidentally
brushed your teeth
with Preparation H.

Your mantra is
"fast, temporary relief."

Having fun is work.

You've been on more than a dozen
second-honeymoons.

You enjoy the fact that your pacemaker sets off the alarm at airport security gates.

You run to answer
the phone when it rings
—on television.

You only go to the movies
in the afternoon.

Getting from your bed to the
bathroom is like scaling
Mount Everest.

You consider playing Bingo to be a wild night on the town.

You know the words to
"Jeepers Creepers."

College students look like
twelve-year olds.

You've found yourself unable to remember your own name.

You've outlived banks that
turned you down for credit.

Events that happened two months ago
seem like two weeks ago.

You dislocated your hip while
unloading the dishwasher.

You need help getting up
from the couch.

When you go on vacation, you can't remember whether your hotel is the Hyatt, Hilton, or Holiday Inn— because they all begin with letter H.

You've mixed Geritol with vodka.

You remember when kids
walked to school.

You fell for Orson Wells'
War of the Worlds.

You have no idea what e-mail is.

You have no idea why your grandchildren are named Brittany, Amber, Janelle, Dakota, and Tyler.

You comb your eyebrows with a rake.

Your vocabulary includes the word
"spry."

You remember when the word
"hardware" meant hammers,
screw drivers, and pliers.

You can see the writing on the wall,
but you need bifocals to read it.

No one will issue you a
life insurance policy.

You wear loafers because you once reached down to tie your shoelaces and threw out your back for a week.

You chug Mylanta.

You consider history books
"current events."

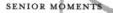

You've actually listened to your children's advice.

When you talk to yourself
you have to turn up
your hearing aid.

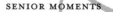

A refrigerator is a "Frigidaire,"
a tissue is a "Kleenex,"
and a kilometer is a "click."

You know who the "King of Swing,"
"The Great Gildersleeve," and
"Mrs. Quackenbush" were.

Your remember the draft.

Your glasses are thick enough to
fry ants.

You can draw the Eiffel Tower by connecting the spots on your back.

You've had to march by yourself in the Veterans of Foreign Wars parade for the last five years.

Your golf clubs are older than Tiger Woods.

You look your age—and then some.

When a bell goes off in your house,
you're not sure if it's the phone,
the door, or that constant ringing
in your ears.

You forgot to feed your dog
because you forgot you had a dog.

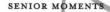

Everyone remembers your birthday
because you've had so many.

You're on a first name basis with the
gardeners at Forest Lawn.

If it's age before beauty,
you are first in line.

You have no ass.

If there's a movie you want to see,
you don't wait for it
to come out on video.

If someone farts in the elevator,
everyone looks at you.

You know that on
the next pain-free day you have,
you'll be wearing your best suit
and someone will be saying a eulogy.

When you are fishing, you hope
you don't catch anything.

Last year you went a little crazy and skipped the annual flu shot.

You won the 80-and-over doubles tournament because the other team couldn't find the tennis courts.

As far as you can tell,
every bottle has a child-proof cap.

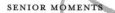

Everyone thinks you're deaf
—but the truth is,
you're really not interested.

You're down to three foods
you can digest.

Your smile is in a glass of water
by the bed.

Your doctor and daughter talk about you as if you aren't even there.

When you tell people
"I've never felt better in my life!"
you know you are lying
and they know you are lying.

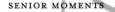

You've been driven around
a mall parking lot
in a security cart
to search for your car.

You've had an MRI,
a CAT scan, and a barium
—because you had nothing better to do.

You're afraid of
your answering machine.

You refuse to drive anything but
a luxury car.

You go to bed at 9 o'clock
and get up at 4:30 A.M.

You have no need for birth control.

You know who the Axis powers were.

You drive ten miles below the speed
limit in the fast lane.

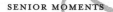

You know all the best places to
gamble with nickels.

You're older than your best bowling score.

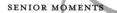

The type in this book
is way too small.

You're older than
any bottle of wine
in France.

You accidentally voted for
Pat Buchanan.

When you went to buy a bikini,
the sales help burst out laughing.

You've fallen and you can't get up.

You still think Bobby Darin, Fabian, and Frankie Avalon are dreamboats.

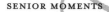

The only thing you do spontaneously
any more is sneeze.

You know who
Kukla, Fran, and Ollie were.

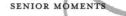

The only exercise you get is using the TV remote control.

When you see a grandmother with
her teenaged grand-daughter,
you get the hots for
the grandmother.

Your children have gone gray.

You remember life before
Scotch tape.

You figure that Hugh Hefner
has five girlfriends
for tax purposes only.

You think the music
kids listen to today
is just noise.

You would like to know
the terms of the deals that
Tom Jones and Tina Turner
have made with the devil.

Just the thought of lifting weights is exhausting.

You'd turn off the lights
to save electricity,
but you just don't have
the energy.

You think the Rolling Stones look like teenagers.

You take your daily medication hourly.

Your stomach has a mind of its own.

The Book-of-the-Month Club
seems more like the
Book-of-the-Week Club.

Although you can't remember
most of your friends' names,
it doesn't matter
because they're all dead anyway.

You've told your kids
not to spank their kids,
even though you
spanked your kids.

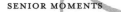

When you get out of the shower,
you're relieved the mirror
is steamed up.

You drive on top of the
dotted white line.

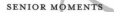

You burn the midnight oil before noon.

The music on the Oldies station is too hip for your tastes.

When it comes to
painting the town red,
you'd rather pay professional
painters to do it for you.

You stuck the cell phone your kid gave you in your sock drawer so it won't make a racket when it rings.

You have handles on the wall
and rubber flowers on the floor
in your bathtub.

You've told toll-booth operators,
sales clerks, and valet parking
attendants about your
grandchildren.

You can no longer see through
a see-through nightgown.

Your wardrobe consists of
several pairs of slippers
with matching bathrobes.

You have disinherited your son on
at least three separate occasions.

You've told the same story to the same person six times.

Your favorite pastime is surfing the Internet medical sites.

You've had more bypasses than
Liz Taylor's had husbands.

You have trouble remembering that
you're losing your memory.

You've come to the realization that
you live in a trailer park in
Palm Beach County.

Your first car was the first car.

You've milked a cow.

You need opera glasses to watch
a soap opera.

You encourage your spouse to go shopping so you can be alone.

You own enough "How To" books
to know you'd rather not
do anything yourself.

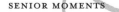

You remember when
Dick Tracy married Tess Trueheart,
when Li'l Abner married Daisy May,
and when Little Ricky was born.

You need an air traffic controller to keep track of your daily medications.

You remember when
Dick Van Dyke
and Andy Griffith
had good TV shows.

The clock on your VCR
has been flashing 12:00
since the Reagan Administration.

The last time you went out on the town was to a CPR class.

You will stop driving when they pry
your cold dead hands off the wheel
of your Seville.

It took you ten years
to get used to being 60.

Advertisers don't care
if you watch their shows.

You can't remember what you did
for a living.

No one has seen your real hair since 1978.

Everyone attends
your birthday party
"because it might be
the last one."

You know who the
"Sultan of Swat" was.

Now that your ship has come in,
you're constantly sea sick.

You attend funerals just to have
something to do.

There's no charge for a ski lift ticket
for your age group.

You're long past the days when
"all-you-can-eat"
is a better deal than
"a la carte."

Every year 20 percent of your holiday
cards come back stamped "deceased."

You still can't understand why all
women over 65 call each other
"girls."

You no longer respect your elders—
because you no longer have any.

You saw *The Jazz Singer* in a movie theater.

You've been saving that flag with forty-eight stars—just in case the Hawaii and Alaska thing doesn't work out.

You're wise enough
to watch your step,
but you need a walker to do so.

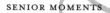

You wear Nike sneakers
but never run anywhere.

You've actually considered
buying a coffin with
a built-in VCR and wet bar.

You've looked for your own name
in the obituaries.

People no longer call you
"sir" or "ma'am."
They call you
"Pops" or "Granny."

You retired and nobody noticed.

You've come to the awful realization that, like youth, you'll also outgrow old age.

You wish you had flossed.

You never buy the "family" size.

You march to the beat of
your own pacemaker.

You know who John Dillinger,
Baby Face Nelson, and Red Grange
were.

No matter what size
underwear you buy,
the waistband always seems to
come up over your navel.

All of your friends are dead
and most of their children are, too.

If you have to allow
four to six weeks for delivery,
you think twice before
placing your order.

You spend most of your leisure time
thinking of ways to screw the
government out of your estate taxes.

You remember where you were when
Garfield was shot.

You still refer to the
phone company as "Ma Bell"
and you still don't know why.

Your train of thought
stops at every station.

You envy your dog's ability
to eat whatever it wants,
sleep whenever it wants,
and pee wherever it wants.

Your third grade lunch box is now worth more than you collected last year in Social Security.

Your line of sight is slowly but surely coming into perfect alignment with the top of your steering wheel.

You choose restaurants based on the cleanliness of the bathroom rather than the ambience of the decor.

You've gotten by
without using an ATM up to now
and you don't see any reason
to start any time soon.

You hardly ever use your credit cards
and you never carry a balance.

You describe your car as
"bought and paid for."

Half the countries
in Europe and Africa
didn't exist when
you were born.

You're not getting older,
you're dead.